THIS CANDLEWICK BOOK BELONGS TO:

_____

_____

_____

_____

First U.S. paperback edition in this form 1994.

The illustrations in this book first appeared in
My First Book of Numbers by Rosalinda Kightley (pp 12-13, 32-3);
My First Book of Puzzles by Charlotte Knox (pp 18-19, 42-3);
My First Book of Words by Julie Lacome
(pp 8-9, 14-15, 22-3, 28-9, 34-5, 38-9, 46-7, 52-3, 56-7);
My First Book of Animals by Louise Voce
(pp 10-11, 16-17, 20-1, 26-7, 30-1, 40-1, 44-5, 50-1, 54-5, 60-1);
My First Book of Machines by Tony Wells (pp 24-5, 36-7, 48-9, 58-9);
all first published in Great Britain by Walker Books Ltd., London, 1986.

Library of Congress Cataloging-in-Publication Data

My first book : words and pictures for the very young /
Louise Voce . . . [et al.].—1st U.S. ed.
Summary: Labeled illustrations introduce numbers, animals, colors,
sounds, and other familiar things encountered in everyday life.
Features games, picture puzzles, and poems.
ISBN 1-56402-034-7 (hardcover)—ISBN 1-56402-370-2 (paperback)
1. Vocabulary—Juvenile literature. [1. Vocabulary.] I. Voce, Louise.
PE1449.M89   1992
428.1—dc20   91-71831

2 4 6 8 10 9 7 5 3 1

Printed in Hong Kong

Candlewick Press
2067 Massachusetts Avenue
Cambridge, Massachusetts 02140

my first book

picture puzzles and word fun
for the very young

Louise Voce

by

Rosalinda Kightley

Tony Wells

Charlotte Knox

Julie Lacome

CANDLEWICK PRESS

CAMBRIDGE, MASSACHUSETTS

An introduction to My First Book

This isn't really *my* first book at all: it's *your* first book. You might like to write your name on the bookplate at the front of the book!

You can enjoy your book in any way you want. Everyone is different and they like to do things in different ways. You can start at the beginning and go through the middle to the end, or you can start at the end and go backward, or you can turn straight to the pages you like best. You can listen and look (if someone will read to you), or you can read aloud, or you can read without making any noise at all.

The following guide will help you to find your favorite pages:

Skipping's hot, ice cream's cool,

splish, splash, splosh in my wading pool.

hand

elbow

shoulder

tummy

bottom

leg

foot

Help the babies find their mothers,

cat

horse

sheep

gosling

tadpole

hen

baby kangaroo

calf

dog

lioness

first the chick, then all the others.

frog

kangaroo

lion cub

puppy

foal

lamb

kitten

chick

goose

cow

Would you like to share a picnic

with a bear or two?

A castle on the sand,

boat

kite

sun

flag

sun hat

ice cream

beach ball

sand castle

seashells

pail

shovel

inner tube

ice cream in my hand.

umbrella

beach chair

ocean

crab

towel

beach bag

picnic

starfish

The sea is where we like to be.

shark

turtle

squid

whale

eel

lobster

dolphin

fish

sea horse

starfish

octopus

The rain pours down, the sky grows dark.

Can you name the animals in the ark?

These are a little like the cats you know.

leopards

lynx

lion

lioness

Would you dare to pet them though?

cheetah

tiger

puma

jaguar

Crayons and paints, red, yellow, blue,

pink   blue   orange   white   green

all the colors belong to you.

gray   red   yellow   black   purple

The sun and the rain will ripen the grain.

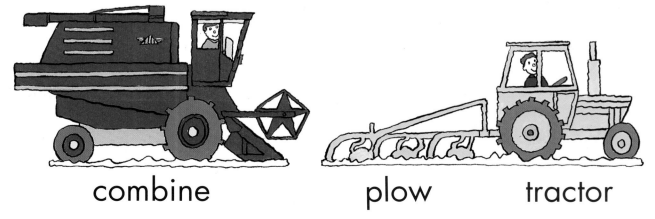

combine   plow   tractor

trailer

pickup truck

25

A moment's calm on the farm.

rooster

sheep

donkey

goat

turkey

chicken

pigs

horse

cows

ducks

bull

Bread and cheese?
Cherries, please.

carrots

bread

bananas

jam

cupcake

tomatoes

eggs

peas

cookie

fish

cheese

cherries

orange juice

apples

hamburger

Who eats carrots, who eats fish?

a frog eats...

an anteater eats...

a squirrel eats...

a pelican eats...

a sheep eats...

What is the panda's favorite dish?

a rabbit eats...

a hen eats...

a crow eats...

a panda eats...

bees eat...

a dog eats...

How many girls? How many boys?

How many flowers? How many toys?

Stroll along the sidewalk, watch the busy street,

tricycle

motorcycle

car

lots and lots of wheels—
not many feet.

store

sidewalk

bus

bicycle

pickup truck

Pick up your wrench,
your hammer and jack;

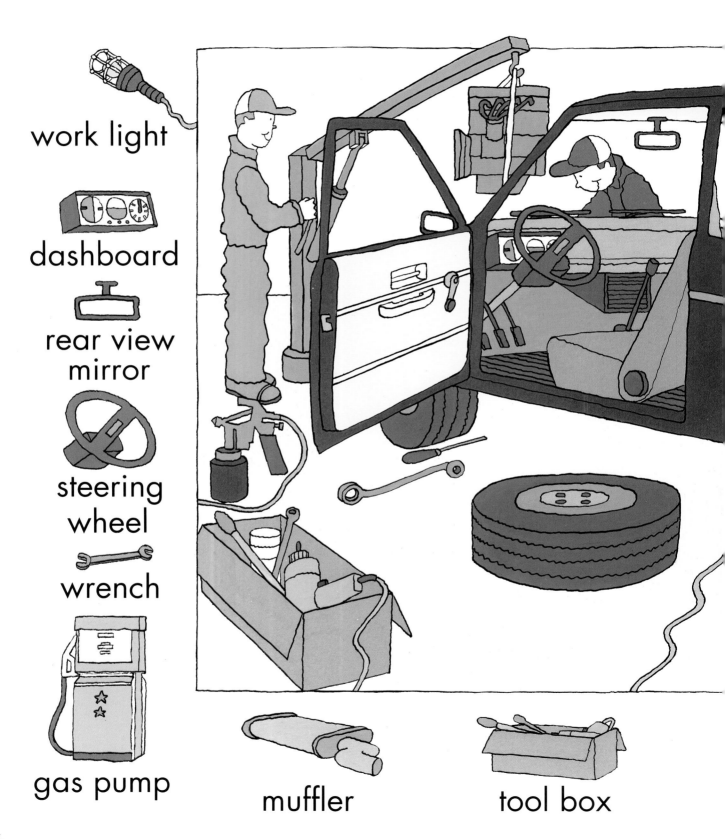

work light

dashboard

rear view
mirror

steering
wheel

wrench

gas pump

muffler

tool box

take the car apart, then put it all back.

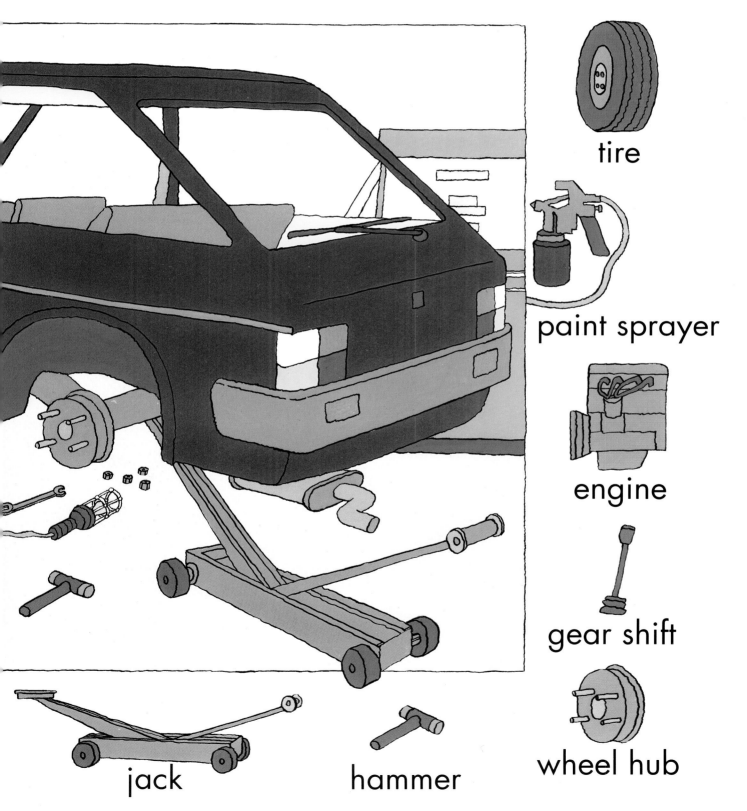

tire

paint sprayer

engine

gear shift

wheel hub

jack

hammer

Do you have a teddy bear, yo-yo, or ball?

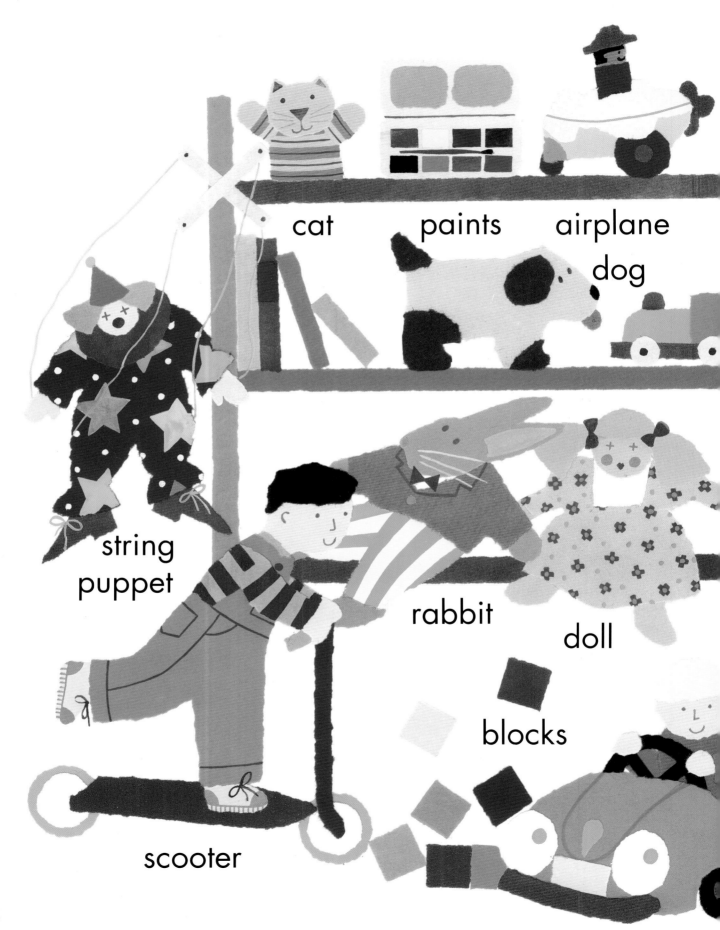

cat

paints

airplane

dog

string
puppet

rabbit

doll

blocks

scooter

Which is your favorite toy of all?

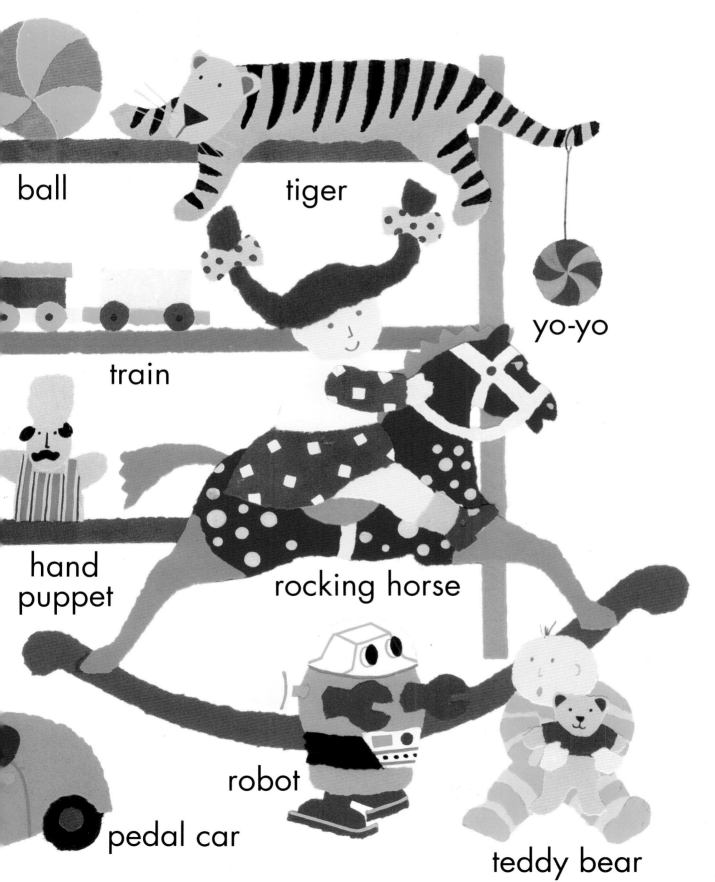

ball

tiger

yo-yo

train

hand
puppet

rocking horse

robot

pedal car

teddy bear

Jungle prowlers, howlers, growlers....

howler monkeys

spider monkeys

armadillo

anteater

jaguar

hummingbird

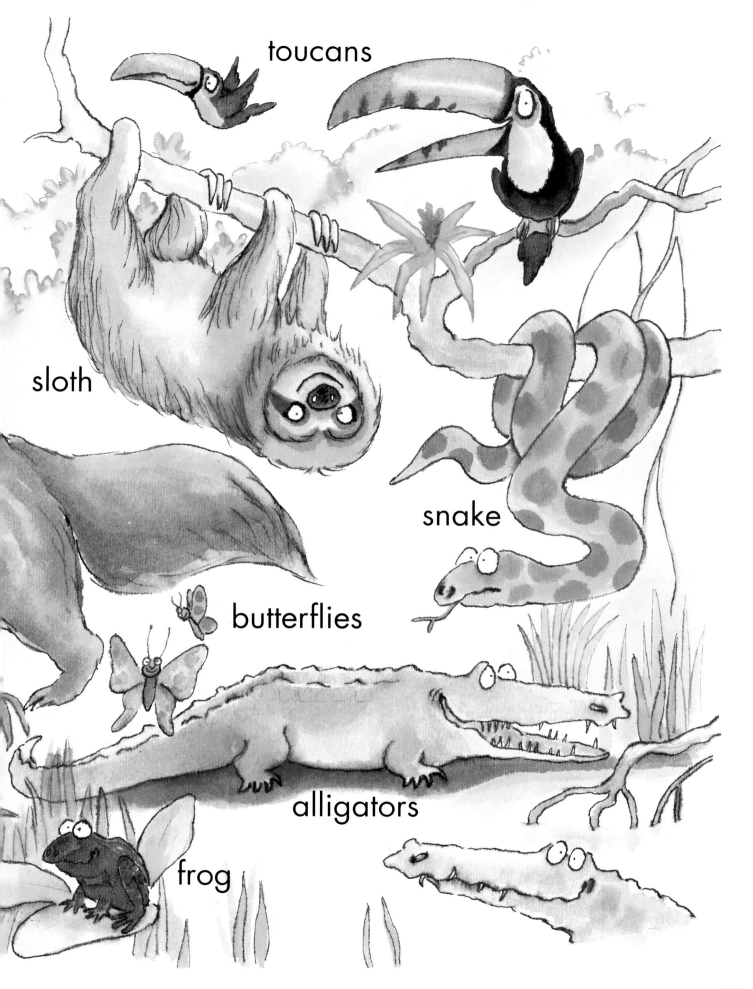

toucans

sloth

snake

butterflies

frog

alligators

Slither and hiss, slither and hiss,

how many heads and tails in this?

Squeaking's just one way of speaking.

neigh

woof

baaaa

quack

squeak

hee-haw

oink

croak

squawk

roar

cluck

meow

moOoo

hissssssss

Sometimes I...

run

read

cry

splash

dance

drink

eat

swing

fall

laugh

jump

sleep

47

Big wheels, little wheels, spinning around,

crane

van

motorcycle

tanker

with a rattle or a whirr or a roaring sound.

car carrier

car

go-cart

bus

Who would you like to live at your house?

dog

hamster

goldfish

gerbil

rabbit

A clumsy big dog? A tiny brown mouse?

mouse

guinea pig

parakeet

turtle

cat

If you were to work instead of play,

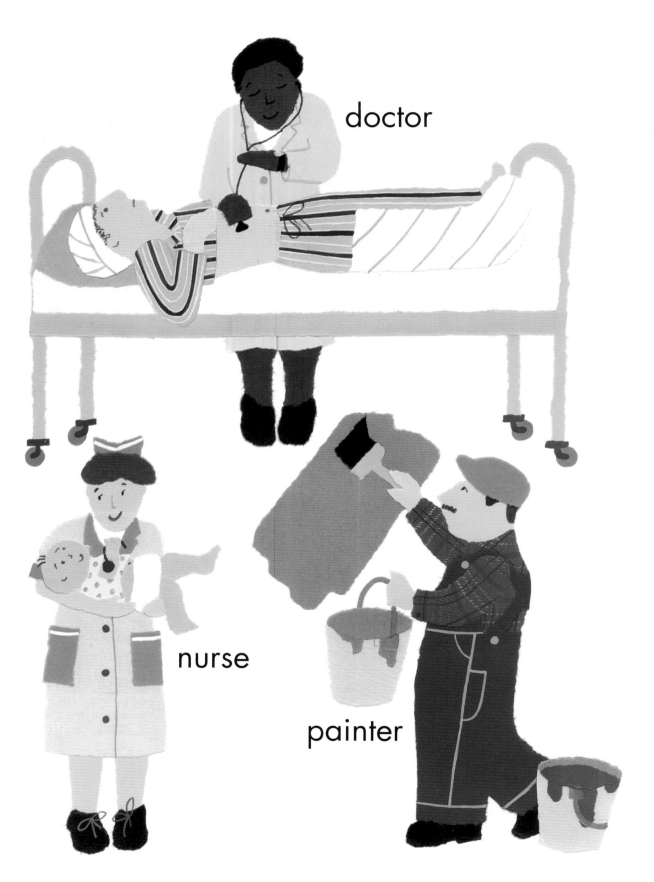

doctor

nurse

painter

what would you like to be all day?

repairman

cook

builder

veterinarian

We think snow and ice are nice.

penguins

walrus

seals

wolf

musk-ox

54

polar bear

sea lion

arctic fox

reindeer

55

I might wear shorts, or jeans instead,

socks

dress

T-shirt

sweater

shoes

pants

or put on pajamas and go back to bed.

pajamas

hat

shorts

shirt

jeans

boots

Flying up high, into the sky.

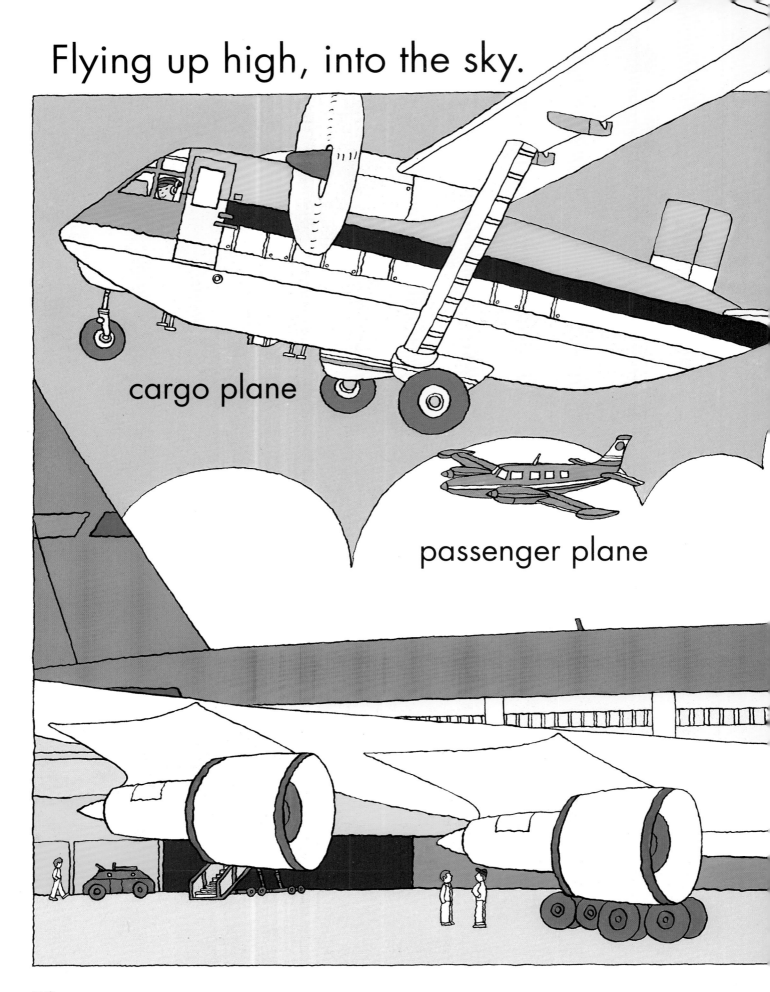

cargo plane

passenger plane

balloon

blimp

helicopter

jet

59

East or west, home is best.

birds' nest

squirrels' nest

anthills

beaver lodge

wasps' nest

spider web

mole tunnel

bear cave

rabbit burrow

mouse hole

61